WINDOWS OF WO...

grace

grace

WINDOWS OF WORSHIP™

When I'm
NEEDING a FRESH START

:: DEVOTIONAL JOURNAL ::

Greg Allen ▪ Rick Rusaw ▪ Dan Stuecher
Paul S. Williams, *Editor*

Standard
PUBLISHING

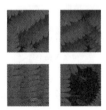

© 2004 CNI Holdings Corp., Windows of Worship is a Trademark of
Christian Network, Inc.

Published by Standard Publishing, Cincinnati, Ohio. A division of Standex
International Corporation. Printed in China.

Cover and interior design by Rule29.

Discover where to watch *Worship* in your town by logging on to
www.Worship.net.

ISBN 0-7847-1518-1

09 08 07 06 05 04   9 8 7 6 5 4 3 2 1

We were made to worship...

The first song I remember Grandma Stone singing to me was "Jesus Loves Me." As a three-year-old I sat on her lap on the front porch swing and asked her to sing it over and over again. Before my daughter Jana could speak, she hummed the same tune, its melody unmistakable as she played on the family room floor. We were made to worship.

To worship God is to walk through the shadows into a familiar welcoming place, where the fire never dies and the light is soft and glowing. To worship God is to know we are truly home, acting on a desire deep in our souls. Long before we rationally understand the truth of Christ, we want to praise someone or something for bringing love and beauty, joy and hope into the world.

At the Christian Network, our desire is simple. Whether through the written page or the television screen, we hope these words and images will draw you to worship, as we thank our creator for breathing life and love into his creation.

PAUL S. WILLIAMS

Chairman of the Board of Stewards
The Christian Network, Inc.

A Better Story

> [Jesus said,] "Enter through the narrow gate. For wide is the gate and broad is the road that leads to destruction, and many enter through it. But small is the gate and narrow the road that leads to life, and only a few find it."
>
> MATTHEW 7:13, 14

A BETTER STORY

If you live in North America, Europe, Australia, or New Zealand, then you are a part of what is called the Western world. Western civilization was born in Greece and Rome around the time of Christ. For the better part of the next 1,500 years, most of Western civilization embraced the Christian story, believing mankind existed to bring praise, honor, and glory to God. If you imagine all of life as a television set, then it didn't much matter to what channel you turned the old television set—all you got was the "God channel." Christianity was the only real channel in town. It was the dominant religion, at the forefront of an entire civilization. And it all started on the shores of the Mediterranean.

But then, about the time Columbus sailed to America, a little over 500 years ago, the Modern Age was born: the age of enlightenment. There was still a strong belief in God, but now there was a second competing channel emerging to challenge the predominant God channel. The Modern Age brought into being the "Science channel." The Science channel said mankind would be able to set himself free from God through rational scientific understanding. That channel reigned for the better part of the next 500 years as we built up hope in man's rational powers and our ability to make sense of life without any need for God.

Now, that age too is coming to an end. Science simply can't provide all the answers we hoped for. It cannot explain the meaning of life. Science offers no purpose for life. And now we no longer have two competing channels, God and Science. Now we've entered a new era, the Postmodern Age.

The Postmodern Age is a channel-surfing culture, with 500 different channels each vying to explain the meaning of life. If the traditional Judeo-Christian view isn't your cup of tea, and science can't explain the meaning of life, then we'll each have to create our own meaning for our own lives. For one person, it might be traditional Christianity. For another, it's the New Age movement. For yet another, it's the ecology movement, or gross material-ism, or an Eastern religion. No one worldview is true for all in the postmodern world. There is only "what's true for me."

But in the midst of such confusing clatter, we as Christians believe there is a better way. There is one channel for everyone— it's the best channel, the best story. This story has 2,000 years of history behind it. Christianity is not the new religion on the block. It has stood the test of time. Oh sure, it's shown some major cracks throughout its 2,000-year history. The Crusades weren't anything to write home about, and religious intolerance still rears its ugly head sometimes. But through it all stands a single magnificent person who stops our channel surfing mid click—Jesus of Nazareth. This one man changed everything.

If you are a Christian, you are a part of a community whose roots go back to the focal point of history—to Jesus Christ, risen from the grave. You are not a part of the religion of Hollywood or the spiritual-idea-of-the-month club. You are of the lineage of Peter and John, Augustine and John of the Cross, Thomas Aquinas and Martin Luther, Teilhard de Chardin and John Wycliffe, Dietrich Bonhoeffer and Dorothy Day. You follow a long line of travelers who have gone before you on the journey. For over 2,000 years a community of believers called the church has committed itself to living as Jesus would have us live.

So when the day is through and all the tales have been told, you must choose a "channel." And the one that tells of Jesus is the channel to which I choose to stay tuned.

—*Paul S. Williams*

What "channels" are vying for your attention? How do they
compare with Jesus and his message?

Are you tuning in to the other "channels" more than you are focusing on Jesus? What might you do to refocus yourself on Christ and his love for you?

9

Amazing Grace

The earth is the LORD's, and everything in it,

the world, and all who live in it;

for he founded it upon the seas

and established it upon the waters.

Who may ascend the hill of the LORD?

Who may stand in his holy place?

He who has clean hands and a pure heart,

who does not lift up his soul to an idol

or swear by what is false.

He will receive blessing from the LORD

and vindication from God his Savior.

Such is the generation of those who seek him,

who seek your face, O God of Jacob.

PSALM 24:1-6

AMAZING GRACE

It has been my privilege to serve on the board of directors of a nonprofit company that operates homes for individuals with developmental disabilities. I have been wonderfully impressed with the people who provide care for the residents of those homes. They are marvelous caregivers who are deeply concerned about each resident.

There is grounding in that kind of service, whether it is paid or volunteer, that provides wisdom. Henri Nouwen, the former Harvard and Yale professor, learned this when he went to work with the Daybreak Community in Toronto, Canada. He received from the residents there a love and acceptance that he had never known before. Maybe that is why thousands of people, for centuries, have called those with developmental disabilities "children of God."

A church in West Virginia warmly invites residents from a home similar to Daybreak to participate in their church services. On one occasion the workers took several residents, including one whose religious background was unknown, to a spiritual retreat. When the workers were ready to depart, shortly before the congregants celebrated the Lord's Supper, one particular resident of the group home refused to leave. When the time came to receive Communion, she insisted on joining in. She didn't talk much, but she obviously understood the Lord's Supper, and she wanted to participate.

The church and the home worked together to disciple this woman, and she later joined the church. Though she rarely spoke at all, on the day that she was welcomed as a member she stood at the front of the church and began to sing. That's right. She began to sing—"Amazing grace, how sweet the sound, that saved a wretch like me. I once was lost, but now I'm found, was blind, but now I see."

That particular woman may in fact have a developmental disability, but there is no mistaking that she understands life's most important truth. The workers, volunteers, and others joined in the song and realized they were all, every last one of them, children of God, privileged to ascend the hill of the Lord and stand in a holy place, with clean hands and pure heart.

In the hills of West Virginia, at a generous church, and in the living room of a home of eight individuals, who just happen to have developmental disabilities, God is known. And he invites *all* who will come to ascend the hill of the Lord.

—Paul S. Williams

When you come across someone with a physical or mental disability, what is your first reaction? Why do you think you react this way?

_____

_____

_____

_____

_____

_____

_____

_____

_____

_____

_____

_____

_____

Because of sin, we are all disabled spiritually, if not physically or mentally. How does that idea change your thoughts about those with outward disabilities? How does it make you feel to know that God's grace makes us all whole again, no matter what our challenges?

_____

_____

_____

_____

15

_____

_____

_____

_____

_____

_____

_____

_____

The Composer at the Door

[Jesus said,] "Here I am! I stand at the door and knock. If anyone hears my voice and opens the door, I will come in and eat with him, and he with me."

REVELATION 3:20

THE COMPOSER AT THE DOOR

"There is no music sweeter to a person than the sound of his or her own name." The first time I heard that quote I remember thinking to myself, *How true it is*. As a minister, part of my job is to love people. I pray it is obvious that I do. In an attempt to express my love for people I make it my business to work hard at remembering their names. In order to do so I employ a variety of disciplines that might surprise you. At nearly every service, I greet someone at church I do not see very often, and I will call him or her by name. The reaction is always fun to watch— the person's countenance changes. There is an instant glimmer in the eye that is a combination of surprise and delight. I can almost hear the person thinking, *He remembered my name.* We all love to be recognized.

But suppose you had achieved what you believed to be a measure of popularity only to discover that hardly anyone knew who you were. Such was the case for one of the world's most beloved composers on a cold, blustery night in a German town where he thought everyone knew his name.

Anyone today would have to be playing dumb not to know the name of Wolfgang Amadeus Mozart. You don't have to be a musician to have heard of him. Over the past 200 years, count- less books have been written about him, and concert perform- ances by the thousands have presented selections from his vast repertoire of over 650 compositions. Modern recordings of his music are beyond number. Albert Einstein proclaimed, "As an artist or a musician, Mozart was not a man of this world." For the student of music the name Mozart is a household word.

But it was not always so, especially during the brief span of Mozart's 35 years of life. Cultured Europe in the late 18th century could be an extremely fickle audience. Even a musical genius like Mozart could be the toast of the town one night and all but forgot- ten the next. Very few pieces of his music were even published during his lifetime. Near the end of his life, when his popularity should have been at its greatest, he returned to the town of Mannheim where he had lived some years before because he knew his opera, *Figaro*, was being performed there. Late in the evening when he arrived at the concert hall where rehearsals were being conducted, he went to the door of the theater and knocked. After some moments an actor answered, obviously irritated with the interruption, and Mozart asked if he might be allowed to listen to the rehearsal of the great opera. The actor was annoyed. He mistakenly thought the visitor was a tailor's apprentice and abruptly told him to get lost.

"Surely, you will allow Mozart to listen to Mozart, will you not?" said the composer. It was only then that the actor did indeed recognize the man standing before him, and with great embarrassment, he opened the door so Mozart could come in and listen to the music he had written.

19

Mozart's experience of being shunned is really nothing in the light of Christ's experience. Jesus, God's Son, is refused entry all the time into hearts that he has created and designed for his residence. In a graphic word picture he describes it something like this: "I'm standing out here knocking on the door. If you recognize me and open it, I'll come in, and we'll have dinner together like the friends we're intended to be" (Revelation 3:20). And why would he be standing out there? Because we have yet to let him in.

I suppose it would be one thing not to know he's outside your heart trying to get your attention. But it would be quite another to know he's there and refuse him entry into the life he's given you to share with him. So go ahead, open the door. You've never heard such music.

—*Dan Stuecher*

How do you feel when someone remembers your name or rec-ognizes you because of some achievement of yours? Why do you think it makes you feel that way?

How do you feel when someone doesn't remember you when you think they should? Have you ever thought about how Jesus feels as he stands outside someone's heart, longing to come in and love that person? Have you let Jesus in?

Sam's Hope

Jesus answered her, "If you knew the gift of God and who it is that asks you for a drink, you would have asked him and he would have given you living water."

"Sir," the woman said, "you have nothing to draw with and the well is deep. Where can you get this living water? Are you greater than our father Jacob, who gave us the well and drank from it himself, as did also his sons and his flocks and herds?"

Jesus answered, "Everyone who drinks this water will be thirsty again, but whoever drinks the water I give him will never thirst. Indeed, the water I give him will become in him a spring of water welling up to eternal life."

JOHN 4:10-14

SAM'S HOPE

I really liked the movie *Pretty Woman.* Not because of Julia Roberts and Richard Gere, but because of the story line. Julia Roberts played the part of a prostitute who was swept away into a totally unexpected adventure. Richard Gere played an extremely successful and wealthy business tycoon who was tired of shallow relationships with women who only wanted his company because of his money. Richard and Julia found in each other a relationship neither expected but both wanted.

This woman went from being victimized to being valued and cherished as a human being and friend. This man went from being alone to having someone to share a life with. There were real conversations, laughter, and peace. I like it when a movie knowingly or unknowingly uncovers God's design for relationships—two human beings who look beyond themselves to meet the needs of another. It's called love.

I loved how Richard Gere and Julia Roberts found a meaningful relationship with one another when neither expected it. But I know of a better story. We'll call the woman Samantha and the man Jesus. Samantha had been divorced five times and was living with a sixth man when she met Jesus. She tried to keep the conversation superficial but he went deeper. She talked water to drink; he talked water of life. She talked about the place to worship; he talked of its purpose. Mostly, she was trying to find meaning in life through relationships with men, and he came to offer her a relationship with God. When Jesus came into her life, he changed everything.

You can spend a lifetime looking for love—through six fallen relationships and more. Or you can find that one special relationship that changes everything. When Samantha went out to the well in the desert that afternoon, she didn't know her life was about to change forever. She had spent a lifetime trying to find the right relationship. She had already gone through five marriages, and was working on her sixth, when Jesus came into her life. He was the seventh man. Did you know that the number seven is the number of perfection in the Bible? When Samantha finally met Jesus, she had found the perfect love—not romantic love, but eternal love. What she found was not someone she could manipulate, but someone who could take her pain away. When Samantha found Jesus, she found the one man whose love could take her all the way to eternity.

—Greg Allen

Where have you been looking for love? Have you found love that satisfies you? Why or why not?

_____

_____

_____

_____

_____

_____

_____

_____

_____

_____

_____

_____

_____

Write a prayer, asking Jesus to bring you that love you're longing for. Pour out your heart to him. He promises to give you the living water of his love and salvation!

_____

_____

_____

_____

_____

_____

_____

_____

_____

_____

_____

_____

_____

Atlantis Rising Up Out of the Sea

In [Christ] we have redemption through his blood, the forgiveness of sins, in accordance with the riches of God's grace that he lavished on us with all wisdom and understanding.

EPHESIANS 1:7, 8

ATLANTIS RISING UP OUT OF THE SEA

The renowned author, Frederick Buechner, tells of the momentous occasion when the grace of God came flooding into his life. A minister was comparing the coronation of Queen Elizabeth to the coronation of Jesus in the heart of a believer. The minister defined it as a time of confession and tears and great laughter. It was the "great laughter" that Buechner said brought the "Great Wall of China crumbling down and Atlantis rising up out of the sea"—an incredible revelation in his heart.

Buechner calls that moment the "crazy holy grace [that] wells up from time to time through flaws and fissures in the bedrock harshness of things." I welcome that grace.

My wife, Cathryn, is a third-grade public school teacher on Long Island, New York. She talks freely with her students about grace. Early in the school year they respond with puzzled looks and raised hands. It seems most of Cathryn's students have never heard the term. But by the time the school year is over, they understand well what it means to be touched by grace.

I was in the classroom one day when Taylor, a student well known in the principal's office, was called to Cathryn's desk. Taylor often made decisions that were neither in his own best interest nor, unfortunately, in the best interest of the entire class. He spent a lot of time at his teacher's desk.

Cathryn had developed a special bond with Taylor. It appeared to me that she understood him in a way few had before. As Taylor approached her desk, without a word he held out his hand as if he were a traffic policeman telling a car to stop. Cathryn held her hand in the same way, and the two hands came together. With finger against finger, she said, "You promised me you wouldn't disrupt the class again. And now you've broken your promise. We had a pact, and you broke it, and I am very disappointed."

Then with fingers still touching fingers, Cathryn went on to say, "What do you think I should do?" A very contrite Taylor looked up at her for a long time and finally answered, "I hope you will show me grace, Mrs. Williams." She did. Cathryn sent Taylor back to his seat unpunished, full of the relief that accompanies amazing grace.

"A crazy holy grace [that] wells up from time to time through flaws and fissures in the bedrock harshness of things," so says Frederick Buechner. Where judgment and criticism were antic- ipated, a forgiving spirit is encountered instead. Where nothing but an empty horizon is expected, a tropical oasis comes into view; and through grace, dry cracked lips drink to their delight. When one tastes of that grace, walls do come tumbling down, islands do rise out of the sea, and it is indeed a time of confession and tears and great laughter.

—*Paul S. Williams*

Can you remember a moment in your life when the understanding of the grace of God came to you in a powerful way?
What does the idea of grace mean to you?

Have you ever experienced grace as given by another person?
Or have you chosen to give grace to another? Reflect here on
your experiences with and feelings about amazing grace.

33

No Longer Victims

[Jesus said,] "And when you stand praying, if you hold anything against anyone, forgive him, so that your Father in heaven may forgive you your sins."

Mark 11:25

NO LONGER VICTIMS

Recently I saw someone who had wronged me a very long time ago. I forgave this person well over a decade ago. But when I saw him, I realized forgiving does not necessarily mean forgetting. Sometimes the memory of a wound stays with us for a lifetime.

On the underside of my left forearm I have a tiny scar from the time my pet rabbit scratched me 40 years ago. Some scars stay with us forever. But it's seldom the physical scars that cause us problems. It's the emotional scars that stay with us the longest, and the people who inflict those wounds are the hardest to forgive.

Forgiveness is a marvelous act. It changes the way we remember a wound. When we have forgiven someone for wounding us, not only do we free the offender from his or her offense, we also free ourselves from the anger that can destroy us. When we forgive a person for harming us, we also give up seeing ourselves as victims of events over which we have no control. The balance of power shifts to us. We become the ones with the final power over a painful memory.

To forgive means to no longer be content to remain a victim. Forgiveness allows us to gain power over painful events and not let those events destroy us. It enables painful memories to be remembered, not for their pain, but for the wisdom they bring.

Forgiveness may not erase painful memories from our lives. But forgiveness will heal the scars of those old wounds; and though the scars might still be visible, they will no longer define our lives.

—*Paul S. Williams*

Are there people who have hurt you that you still haven't forgiven? Who are they? Why can't you forgive?

_____

_____

_____

_____

_____

_____

_____

_____

_____

_____

_____

_____

How might *you* change if you allowed yourself to forgive?

_____

_____

_____

_____

_____

_____

_____

_____

_____

_____

_____

_____

_____

Write a prayer, asking God's help to forgive those who have hurt you. Ask him for healing in your own heart as well.

_____

_____

_____

_____

_____

_____

_____

_____

_____

_____

_____

_____

_____

The Hound of Heaven

[Jesus said,] "You did not choose me, but I chose you and appointed you to go and bear fruit—fruit that will last."

JOHN 15:16

THE HOUND OF HEAVEN

I don't know many people who reason their way to Christianity.
I don't know many people who say, "Well, I think I'll begin a
serious study on whether or not the scientific evidence exists to
prove Jesus Christ was raised from the dead." It's not that that
isn't a good question to ask. It's just that I don't know anyone
who has become a Christian based on finding the answer to that
question. So what, then, *does* compel people to come to Christ?

One of the brightest Christians I know said not long ago, "I never
really pursued God a single day of my life. But everywhere I
turned, I kept finding God pursuing me." There's even a great
poem by Francis Thompson called *The Hound of Heaven*. It's
about God on a relentless search for buried treasure.

I would have to admit, that is how I have experienced God. For
long periods of time, the last thing in the world I was looking for
was God. But then, just like that, there we stood—nose to nose.
He found me. Some people call that moment an epiphany.
Others call it the "aha" revelation. My experience has more
often been of the "oh no" variety, because I realize, now that
God has found me, he's likely to ask something of me. And you
know what? He does.

God asks me to worship him. That's all. Nothing more. Nothing less. But that feels natural, because long before I ever accepted God into my life, I intuitively felt the need to worship someone or something—to say thanks for the good for which I couldn't find any other explanation. Something deep inside me has always wanted to worship the author of all things good, whoever he might be.

I serve as a host on an overnight Christian worship show. Christians haven't always done so well using the medium of television. We often make ourselves look silly and one-dimensional. Worse yet, we make God look silly and one-dimensional. But on our show we've been trying to keep it simple. Sometimes we succeed. Sometimes we don't. But our desire is as basic as our programming. All we want to do is create an environment in which you can find yourself in the presence of the holy one, caught by the hound of Heaven, worshiping him. And if we've done that even once in a great while, then we're doing something right.

—*Paul S. Williams*

What are some of the characteristics of a hound? Relentless in its search? Eager to find? Write out some of these qualities.

Now think about God in terms of the characteristics of a hound that you listed. God is like a hound in his pursuit of you! What are your thoughts and feelings about that idea?

Ingersoll

The world and its desires pass away, but the man who does the will of God lives forever.

1 JOHN 2:17

INGERSOLL

He was one of the most captivating speakers in the history of the United States. More people recognized him than any other American who had not been president. His death in 1899 was one of the most widely noted events in the world. Papers in the United States, Canada, Mexico, Europe, and Africa printed portions of his many writings in tribute. Most everyone agreed that the fame of this man, Colonel Robert Green Ingersoll, was forever secure. Yet today, very few have ever heard of him. Even more remarkable is that the purpose of Ingersoll's crusades, to which thousands gathered, was not to inspire faith in God, but to kill it.

The "Great Agnostic," Robert Green Ingersoll, was a decorated Union colonel from the Civil War. He said, "We are looking for the time when . . . REASON . . . shall be the King of Kings, and God of Gods." Someone predicted upon Ingersoll's death in 1899 that during the 20th century "temples will be built to him, and his image will be worshiped, when all gods and religions . . . shall have been forgotten." The closest thing to a temple might be his birth home, which stands today as a museum in upstate New York. It is the colonel, not God, who is forgotten. And yet, there is at least one unforgettable contribution for which Robert Ingersoll *can* be held responsible.

Once, on a train ride, Robert Ingersoll spent several hours with a Union general, giving a persuasive presentation as to why someone should not believe in Jesus Christ. Up to this point the general had been indifferent about religion. But Ingersoll was so eloquent that his fellow traveler was compelled to investigate. The result of General Lew Wallace's research was a novel. And though you may never have heard of Robert Green Ingersoll, you have likely heard of *Ben-Hur*, Lew Wallace's story of a Roman slave's journey to faith.

—Eric Snyder for Greg Allen

Why do you think the story of *Ben-Hur* remains such a classic, while the writings of Robert Ingersoll have not continued in their fame as some predicted?

_____

_____

_____

_____

_____

49

_____

_____

_____

_____

_____

_____

_____

_____

What stories of faith have remained with you throughout your life? Sunday school Bible stories? Books or movies? Stories your parents or grandparents told you? Why do you think they have remained with you?

What stories of faith can you pass on to the next generation?
Write down some ideas and plan to share your stories.

_____

_____

_____

_____

_____

_____

_____

_____

_____

_____

_____

_____

_____

_____

Reaping a Whirlwind

Those who sow in tears

    will reap with songs of joy.

He who goes out weeping,

    carrying seed to sow,

will return with songs of joy,

    carrying sheaves with him.

PSALM 126:5, 6

REAPING A WHIRLWIND

James Carter (no relation to our former president) was the son
of a Mississippi sharecropper. At the age of 13 he ran away from
home. What followed was a series of arrests and convictions—
twice for stealing, once for a parole violation, and once for
a weapons offense. On four occasions he served time in the
Mississippi State Penitentiary. In those days that meant working on a chain gang, doing backbreaking labor under a blazing
Mississippi sun. Everyone knows "you reap what you sow," and
James Carter had sown for himself a life of misery. But on
a mid-September day in 1959, in shackles and chains—the consequences of his actions—this wayward son sowed to the wind.
As a result of that September day, over 50 years later he would
reap a joyful whirlwind.

James Carter was 76 years old and living in a poor neighborhood
in Chicago when he received an unexpected knock at his door.
A couple of investigators had come to speak to him concerning
something that had happened over 50 years ago. Mr. Carter had
been thought to be dead by now, but due to the Freedom of
Information Act, the investigators, along with the help of a
newspaper reporter, were able to look through the files of the
Mississippi parole board where they found evidence that James
Carter had moved to Chicago in 1967. After painstakingly track-
ing him down, they proceeded to tell him why they were looking
for him. No, he was not in trouble. In fact they had good news.
Good news related to his time spent decades earlier on a
Mississippi chain gang.

On that fateful day in September 1959, James Carter did something that he had often done. To help carry the road crew
through the day, James led them in an old song, which he bel-
lowed to the rhythm of pickaxes. On this day, however, a man
named Alan Lomax brought a tape recorder and captured the
singing as part of a folk music collection representing the
American South. Fifty years later, while collecting music for the
soundtrack to the movie, *O Brother, Where Art Thou?* producer
T-Bone Burnett heard Lomax's recording of James Carter
singing the song "Po Lazarus." The producer was so moved that
he made the recording the opening song of the movie and the
first track on the CD.

The investigators who found Mr. Carter in Chicago were from
the Lomax Archives. They came bearing a check for $20,000,
the first of many checks to be issued for his Grammy winning
performance of "Po Lazarus." No, life sometimes isn't fair, but
for this wayward son, it's more than fair. It's full of grace instead.

—Eric Snyder for Rick Rusaw

Write about a time when you reaped what you sowed—when you had to face the consequences of sinful actions.

_____

_____

_____

_____

_____

_____

_____

_____

_____

_____

_____

_____

Now, write about a time when you received grace and did not have to face the full consequences of your sin. Praise God for his overwhelming grace and forgiveness!

_57_

Noah and Rainbows

God said to Noah and to his sons with him:

"I now establish my covenant with you and with your descendants

after you and with every living creature that was with you—the

birds, the livestock and all the wild animals, all those that came out

of the ark with you—every living creature on earth. I establish my

covenant with you: Never again will all life be cut off by the waters

of a flood; never again will there be a flood to destroy the earth."

And God said, "This is the sign of the covenant I am making

between me and you and every living creature with you, a covenant

for all generations to come: I have set my rainbow in the clouds,

and it will be the sign of the covenant between me and the earth.

Whenever I bring clouds over the earth and the rainbow appears

in the clouds, I will remember my covenant between me and you

and all living creatures of every kind.

GENESIS 9:8-15

NOAH AND RAINBOWS

If you had a good job, wonderful friends, and you loved where you lived, would you move across the country to a strange new place? That's what Danny and Kathie are doing. They are deeply woven into the fabric of their church in Louisville, Kentucky. They have three sons who are precious and well-adjusted. They have great friends and a nice house. And they think they need to move. That's right. They think they need to leave the comforts of home.

But why? Because Danny and Kathie feel they have been called to a life of growth and change. They feel called by God to serve him more fully than ever before. And they are willing to go wherever God wants them to go, whether to a new church in Colorado or an inner-city mission in Atlanta.

As you might expect, they are filled with anxiety. Sometimes they ask themselves, "Are we crazy? We've got everything we need here." But they understand this life is not about amassing quantities of goods and living off the fat of the land. This life is about growing ever deeper in service to others and God. It's about living on the edge with radical faith in Jesus.

Although Danny and Kathie are getting ready to take a big risk in life, they are in good company. Noah had a comfortable life. His family was close by. He had a good job, living off the fat of the land. But then he was called by God to move into new territory—really new territory. He was called to build a boat in the middle of dry ground.

Noah was scared and confused, but he trusted God. Then the rain came, and the rest is history. And as the ship hit dry land many weeks later, and Noah and his family looked up at the rainbow God provided, they understood the reward of a life of trust.

Danny and Kathie don't know exactly what the future holds for them, but they know they've been called by God to grow in their service to him. And they are willing to go wherever God leads. I am confident that wherever they land, they will be fine, and there will be a rainbow, God's promise to provide, waiting for them.

—Greg Allen

Has God ever asked you to do something that seemed to make no sense? Is he asking you to do something "crazy" right now? How do you feel about that?

_____

_____

_____

_____

_____

_____

_____

_____

_____

_____

_____

_____

_____

Throughout human history, God has asked people to do things that made no human sense, but in the end, blessings always followed those who obeyed. Write a prayer, telling God about your fears and misgivings about the things he is asking you to do. Then give them to him, trusting his promise to bless you if you obey.

_____

_____

_____

_____

63

_____

_____

_____

_____

_____

_____

_____

_____

Watching Doomed Sparrows

The Word became flesh and made his dwelling among us.

We have seen his glory, the glory of the One and Only, who came

from the Father, full of grace and truth.

JOHN 1:14

WATCHING DOOMED SPARROWS

Emmanuel—God with us. Where do we begin to understand how or why an omnipotent God, completely free of boundaries, would choose to wrap himself in the limitations of human flesh as an expression of his love . . . for us?

We call it the incarnation. God became a man. There. I said it out loud—but I still don't get it. How can we actually understand what that means?

There is a story told of a man sitting in the kitchen of his farm-house on a raw winter night. He kept hearing an irregular thumping sound against the storm door. He went to the window and watched as tiny, shivering sparrows, attracted to the obvious warmth inside, beat in vain against the glass.

66

In a blend of alarm and compassion the farmer bundled up and trudged through fresh snow to open the barn for the struggling birds. He turned on lights, tossed some hay in a corner, and sprinkled a trail of saltine crackers to direct them to the barn. But the sparrows, having scattered in all directions when he emerged from the house, still hid in the darkness, afraid of him.

He tried circling behind the birds to drive them toward the barn, tossing cracker crumbs in the air toward them. Nothing worked. He stood there, towering over them as a huge alien creature. They were terrified of him. They could not understand that he actually desired to help them.

Concluding there was nothing he could do, the farmer withdrew to the house and watched the doomed sparrows through the window. As he stared, a thought hit him like lightning from a clear blue sky: If only I could become one of them—for just a moment. Then I wouldn't frighten them. I could show them the way to warmth and safety. At that very instant, another thought dawned on him as I'm hoping it's dawning on you. He grasped the meaning of the incarnation: God dwelled among us through his only begotten Son. Just as the farmer would have to become a bird for the sparrows not to fear him, the only way humans could identify with God, and allow him to provide for them what they needed the most, was if God became human.

But a man becoming a bird is nothing compared to God becoming a man. The idea of the God who conceived and created the limitless expanse of our universe choosing to confine himself to a human body—a body that knew poverty, suffering, and sacrifice— why, that's a bit more than some people can believe. But I believe it. Do you?

—Dan Stuecher

67

Have you ever been frustrated trying to communicate with an animal or even a small child? How did you try to make them understand you?

How do you feel when you think about the fact that the God of the universe made himself like you so that you would understand his love?

_____

_____

_____

_____

_____

_____

_____

_____

_____

_____

_____

_____

_____

Nic at Night

Now there was a man of the Pharisees named Nicodemus,

a member of the Jewish ruling council. He came to Jesus at night

and said, "Rabbi, we know you are a teacher who has come from

God. For no one could perform the miraculous signs you are doing

if God were not with him."

In reply Jesus declared, "I tell you the truth, no one can see the

kingdom of God unless he is born again."

"How can a man be born when he is old?" Nicodemus asked.

"Surely he cannot enter a second time into his mother's womb to

be born!"

Jesus answered, "I tell you the truth, no one can enter the kingdom

of God unless he is born of water and the Spirit."

JOHN 3:1-5

NIC AT NIGHT

Gary manages a great little barbecue place with red-checkered tablecloths, a concrete floor, and the absolute best sweet tea. Over time Gary and I have talked enough for him to know that I work at a church and for me to know that he doesn't attend church. But Gary does have a lot of questions—questions like, "So did God cause the terrorist attacks on New York and D.C.?"

As I was lunching on ribs and corn one day Gary said, "I'm 47 years old, and I feel like I'm on a fence, and I have to know what to believe."

Though Gary is a fun guy with a happy outlook, he still wants to know what life's all about. I can hear in his voice and see in his face that he is looking for what all of us are looking for—hope. *Where was God in the terrorist tragedy? In fact, where is God at all? Can you prove I'm not just a cosmic accident? Can you give me hope?*

Even fun people who have positive personalities want to know if there is more—if there is more to life than great barbecue and sweet tea. Jobs crash and family members die with one hijacked airplane. The question is, is there hope for more than this world offers?

That's exactly what Nic wanted to know. Nicodemus was the Gary of the first century. He had a lot of questions about God. But he took his questions straight to the source—Jesus.

One night, when his disapproving peers wouldn't see him, Nic found Jesus and quizzed him. He asked really good questions and made it obvious he was just a man sitting on a fence who needed to know what to believe, just like Gary. Jesus told him, "God so loved the world that he gave his one and only Son, that whoever believes in him shall not perish but have eternal life" (John 3:16). There was Nic's hope. There is Gary's hope. And there is your hope.

Gary is still asking questions. I'm glad. Gary's asking questions about God tells me he has not dropped into apathetic indifference. He knows he needs to get off that fence. Maybe you too are on a fence about God. You're just trying to figure this life out. Well, my friend, I'd like to encourage you. Like Nic and Gary, go ahead and ask the hard questions. God can handle them. It's OK to be sitting on a fence for a spell. But I've got a feeling that, if you ask those questions with all your heart, you won't be on the fence for long.

—Greg Allen

Are you still on the fence about God? Even if you believe in God, you probably still have lots of questions. Write some of your questions below.

_____

_____

_____

_____

_____

_____

_____

_____

_____

_____

_____

_____

_____

Use the concordance in the back of a Bible and do some research on the questions you have. Write down any answers or insights you find. Search out a minister or godly friend who can help you find further answers to your questions.

_____

_____

_____

_____

_____

_____

_____

_____

_____

_____

_____

_____

Listening to the Right Voice

"Whether you turn to the right or to the left, your ears will hear a voice behind you, saying, "This is the way; walk in it," [says the Lord.]

ISAIAH 30:21

LISTENING TO THE RIGHT VOICE

I couldn't have been more than 7 or 8 years old. I was watching
a Walt Disney cartoon featuring one of my favorite characters,
Goofy—if you can believe that. On one shoulder was a small caricature of Goofy as a devil with the red suit, pointed tail, and
a sinister look on his face. On the other shoulder was another
caricature of Goofy as a rather sublime-looking little angel,
complete with wings and halo. They alternately whispered in
Goofy's ear. It was thoroughly entertaining. I remember both
little characters providing advice with which I could relate. Oh,
I knew the little devil was the wrong influence, but what he said
. . . well, it made so much sense. Of course, I knew the little
angel was the right one to listen to because I had heard what he
was saying many, many times. Yeah, it was a cartoon. But it was
also a rather pointed parable about life.

On a remote airstrip almost a half century ago, a small plane was
preparing to taxi into position for takeoff. An unexpected storm
system was approaching with heavy rain and gusty winds. It had
already started raining and the wind was picking up. Suddenly,
a lone figure, with his coat over his head in a futile attempt to
keep dry, ran from the terminal to the plane, his silhouette out-
lined by lightning, the wind now almost tearing his coat from
his grasp. Upon seeing the man on the runway the surprised
pilot shut down the twin engines and opened the door. The man
came on board, had a rather heated exchange with the pilot, and
then turned to the eight passengers. "My name is Walter Beech,"
he said. "I am the designer of this airplane and I supervised its
construction. I know what it can do and what it can't do. This
plane is not designed for weather this severe and I urge you to
get off with me now. I know your destinations are important
and this represents an inconvenience, but please, don't remain
on the plane."

The pilot interrupted angrily. "I have been flying this aircraft
for years and I, too, know what it can do and what it can't do. If

we avoid further delay we can get ahead of this storm. I urge you to stay on board. I will get you to your destinations."

One woman stood and walked forward to get off the plane with Walter Beech. The two watched as the plane left the ground, climbing several hundred feet. Then what began as a slow roll quickly became an ugly, uncontrollable spin as the aircraft fell from the sky. All aboard were lost.

The woman standing with Walter Beech was Eleanor Roosevelt, wife of the President of the United States. She would later tell reporters, "I felt it wise to take the advice of the designer and builder of the airplane."

There are so many voices in life commanding our attention, so many different options from which to choose, so many sources of advice claiming to have the right information. But it is the childhood memory of a Disney cartoon with Goofy listening to a little devil on one shoulder and an angel on the other that brings things into a proper perspective for me. To whom will I listen? Will I give attention to the prevailing philosophies of today, knowing full well they are subject to change tomorrow? Or do I listen to the truth that is unchanging?

Eleanor Roosevelt's life was spared because she listened to the designer of an airplane advising her against flying in poor conditions.

God always sees clearly what is best for us. But there will always be options. There will be those other voices enticing us down paths that may bring immediate gratification, but that may ultimately bring sadness and despair. I urge you to listen to God's advice. He's the designer, the only one who can get you to where you're supposed to be.

—*Dan Stuecher*

What other voices are competing with God's for your attention? Reflect on this and list some things that tempt you to focus on them instead of God's will.

What might the consequences be of listening to voices that are not God's voice? Write down your ideas according to the specific voices you listed on the previous page.

Saving Bernard of Clairvaux

For what I do is not the good I want to do; no, the evil I do not want to do—this I keep on doing. Now if I do what I do not want to do, it is no longer I who do it, but it is sin living in me that does it. . . . Therefore, there is now no condemnation for those who are in Christ Jesus, because through Christ Jesus the law of the Spirit of life set me free from the law of sin and death.

ROMANS 7:19, 20; 8:1, 2

SAVING BERNARD OF CLAIRVAUX

His name was Bernard. He was perhaps the greatest cleric of the 12th century and the most prominent historical figure of the Cistercian order. Bernard was a man of peace. His sweetness and eloquence contributed to his nickname, "the honey-tongued doctor." As the abbot of the monastery in Clairvaux, France, Bernard spent half of each day meditating on the Scriptures, completely immersing himself in the Word of God by not only reading it but also singing it. His songs include such well-known hymns as "O Sacred Head, Now Wounded" and "Jesus, the Very Thought of Thee." Today, he would be regarded as a man without blemish, were it not for the strange existence of yet another 12th century monk who oddly enough had the same name.

There was another monk named Bernard, also from Clairvaux. But rather than remain content with the solitude of the monastery, this Bernard found himself wrapped up in the affairs of the world. He often battled those he considered heretics. He used his fame and power of persuasion to influence the nations of Europe to engage in a holy war, the second of the Crusades, which was fought to "liberate" Jerusalem. It was a bloody and wicked disaster. When the calamity was over he blamed the sinfulness of the crusaders for the failure rather than admit that the whole campaign was a mistake. But even more puzzling than the behavior of this monk was the fact that the Bernard of war and the Bernard of peace were the same man. The man who meditated on the Scriptures half of each day was the man who helped start a war that should never have been fought.

There is much that Bernard of Clairvaux has to offer us. His writings are still regarded as some of the most beautiful ever written, full of profound spiritual insight. But Bernard also made mistakes—major mistakes. Influenced by a violent age, he encouraged the nations of Europe to enter into a crusade that turned out to be a disaster.

And in that I find hope. Because I too, like Bernard, am paradoxically two men. I am a good man, devoted to God, my family, and my work. And I am a foolish man, one who makes bad decisions, absolutely convinced of my rightness, yet entirely wrong. It's this fact that makes the third verse of one of Bernard's hymns, "Jesus, the Very Thought of Thee," that much more meaningful:

O hope of every contrite heart, O joy of all the meek,
To those who fall, how kind Thou art! How good to those who seek!

—*Eric Snyder for Paul S. Williams*

Can you relate to Bernard? Do you sometimes feel as if there are two people inside you—one who wants to do good and the other who wants to do bad? Write down some examples of this struggle in your life.

God has promised that he will always provide a way to escape the temptation of evil (1 Corinthians 10:13). Write out this verse and memorize it. Then write the verse in your own words, putting in the specific temptations that you need God's strength to resist.

_____

_____

_____

_____

_____

_____

_____

_____

_____

_____

_____

_____

_____

_____

Forgiveness with a Twist

Moreover, we have all had human fathers who disciplined us and we respected them for it. How much more should we submit to the Father of our spirits and live! Our fathers disciplined us for a little while as they thought best; but God disciplines us for our good, that we may share in his holiness.

HEBREWS 12:9, 10

FORGIVENESS WITH A TWIST

Daria is a traveler. She would go anywhere tomorrow if someone gave her a ticket. You can imagine her excitement when a friend of the family gave her some frequent flyer miles for a trip to London. Now, this was no ordinary vacation. This was a visit— a long-awaited visit.

Over an extended weekend, Daria's break from university study would take her across the ocean to see her boyfriend, Peter, a student in London. Though very close, they hadn't seen each other in three and a-half months. Daily e-mails and occasional phone calls don't cut it with matters of the heart. They eagerly anticipated the reunion—relishing each stage of its planning. Parents had been consulted and frequent flyer miles accrued so this could all come about. Everything was in place. Then came September 11, 2001.

Life changed in an instant on that day. Daria had planned to fly to London to visit her boyfriend in early October. After much thought, prayer, and discussion, Daria's parents decided it would not be advisable to fly to London so soon after the terror-ist attacks. They dreaded telling her their decision. She planned to come home from school on a late September weekend to pick up her passport. After a nice family lunch, her parents broke the news. To say that Daria was disappointed would be an understatement. Pleading and rationalization didn't work with Mom and Dad. Such strategies don't always cut it with matters of the heart—a parent's heart, that is.

Daria went back to school the next day, one frustrated and downcast young woman. And, of course, Mom and Dad were completely emotionally drained. Normally healthy lines of communication were silent—uncomfortably silent.

Her parents really wished that somehow Daria could understand what they, as parents, were thinking. Then, one Monday evening the phone rang. Daria's father answered. It was his daughter. After days of deep thought she told her Dad, "I decided I was going to forgive you and Mom, but then I realized you didn't need to be forgiven, because you were only doing what you thought was right in the first place."

It was not only a moment of clarity for a 20-year-old, it was also a moment of joy. Daria, true to her name, which means "gift," had given her parents a gift, an occasion to take delight in her.

Henri Nouwen said, "The cup of life is the cup of joy as much as it is the cup of sorrow. Life is the cup in which sorrows and joys, sadness and gladness, are never quite separated."

Daria's parents drank the cup and were refreshed with the grace of their daughter's forgiveness—forgiveness for doing what they thought was right in the first place. I guess you could call it forgiveness, with a twist.

—Florence Blyskal for Paul S. Williams

Have you ever been disappointed by someone's decision, but later you discovered that it was for your good? Or have you had to make a decision that disappointed someone else? Describe the situation and your feelings.

Are there circumstances in your life that are disappointing or unfair that God might be using for your greater good? Reflect on this in writing.

_____

_____

_____

_____

_____

_____

_____

_____

_____

_____

_____

_____

_____

Sand or Rock?

[Jesus said,] "Therefore everyone who hears these words of mine and puts them into practice is like a wise man who built his house on the rock. The rain came down, the streams rose, and the winds blew and beat against that house; yet it did not fall, because it had its foundation on the rock. But everyone who hears these words of mine and does not put them into practice is like a foolish man who built his house on sand. The rain came down, the streams rose, and the winds blew and beat against that house, and it fell with a great crash."

MATTHEW 7:24-27

SAND OR ROCK?

In Annie Proulx's award-winning novel, *The Shipping News*, a family moved to Newfoundland where they renovated an old house that had once belonged to their ancestors. The house had been tethered to logs and dragged across the frozen bay from its first location on another island. But without its original foundation, the house rocked and leaned when the wind blew. To shore up the house, at each corner the family secured strong wire cables to the bedrock.

Now that doesn't seem like a great home maintenance strategy to me. And sure enough, a huge storm pounded the coast and demolished the house. But, of course, anyone could have predicted that. Without a firm foundation, no house can stand.

I'm sure you've heard of the Leaning Tower of Pisa. It isn't supported by cables, but maybe it should be! It too suffers from a weak foundation.

For many years, scholars believed the tower was created to show off architectural skill and grab the attention of the world by seeming to challenge gravity. Recently though, scientists discovered the real reason for the leaning—a foundation of sand, clay, and water. The unstable soil transformed the plan for a stunning tower into a blueprint for disaster.

Engineers have worked to stabilize the tower. They've removed dirt, drained away extra water and installed steam pipes to dry out the remaining soil. Although these massive efforts have helped, the tower will never be straight. Why? Because the original builder chose a poor foundation for the tower in the first place.

In the beginning of the 20th century, the famous architect Frank Lloyd Wright attempted to build an earthquake-proof hotel in Tokyo, a city frequently hit with devastating quakes. Wright set pairs of concrete piles along the length of the foundation walls that would stabilize the building whenever the earth was shaking. The plan worked. In 1923, just after the Imperial Hotel was completed, the Great Kanto earthquake hit Japan, but the Imperial Hotel stood, untouched by serious damage.

You know, Jesus talked about a not-so-bright builder who constructed a house on a sandy foundation and another builder who constructed a house on a foundation of stone. And then the storms came. Note that storms rained down on both builders—the good one and the not-so-good one. It doesn't matter who you are—the storms will come. But one house stood and one house didn't, and just like the Imperial Hotel, the Tower of Pisa, or the house from *The Shipping News*, it was the foundation that made all the difference.

—*Jennifer Taylor for Rick Rusaw*

What is the foundation of your life built on? What do you trust in when the storms batter you?

_____

_____

_____

_____

_____

_____

_____

_____

_____

_____

_____

_____

_____

Has your foundation held in the midst of difficult circumstances?
If you feel that things are falling apart, perhaps you need to
cling to the only true foundation—Jesus. Write a prayer, asking
God to help you build on the rock of his love and salvation.

Real Justice

The LORD is compassionate and gracious,

    slow to anger, abounding in love.

He will not always accuse,

    nor will he harbor his anger forever;

he does not treat us as our sins deserve

    or repay us according to our iniquities.

For as high as the heavens are above the earth,

    so great is his love for those who fear him;

as far as the east is from the west,

    so far has he removed our transgressions from us.

PSALM 103:8-12

REAL JUSTICE

Whoever wrote "Sticks and stones may break my bones, but words will never hurt me" was more than a tad confused. Words hurt. And the scars they leave can be debilitating. What does it take for us to get over our hurts?

When we've been wronged, we want justice to prevail. We want people to get what they deserve. This old Irish prayer captures that spirit:

> *May the people love us;*
> *And if they don't love us,*
> *May the Lord turn their hearts;*
> *And if their hearts won't be turned,*
> *May the Lord turn their ankles,*
> *So we can know them by their limping.*

Now there's a certain kind of justice. But is it healthy justice?

The Old Testament word for *justice* does not mean giving people what they deserve, but giving people what God wants them to have. That's quite different from our typical understanding of justice. But think about it. Throughout the Old Testament, Israel was unfaithful to God over and over again. But over and over, instead of punishing Israel God gave his disobedient nation blessing upon blessing that they didn't deserve. That's because God was practicing his brand of justice—giving people what he wants them to have.

When you have been wronged, it is important to understand the wrong that has been done to you. Forgiveness offered too quickly can be cheap and incomplete. But forgiveness that understands fully the depth of that which needs to be forgiven is quite powerful. It is justice at its finest—not giving people what they deserve, but giving them what God wants them to have: unconditional love.

—*Paul S. Williams*

Write about a time when you were wronged and you wanted that person to "get what he deserved."

_____

_____

                                                                    .

_____

_____

_____

_____

_____

_____

_____

_____

_____

_____

_____

Does realizing that God doesn't give you what you deserve, but instead gives you love and forgiveness, change your thoughts about showing grace and forgiveness to those who "don't deserve it"?

105

Who Is First?

Jesus said, "If you hold to my teaching, you are really my disciples. Then you will know the truth, and the truth will set you free."

JOHN 8:31, 32

WHO IS FIRST?

He was the first president of the United States. Congress voted
to provide the new president with a house and servants and
declared that he "takes precedence of all and every person in
the United States." Under his leadership Congress established
the Treasury Department, adopted the seal of the United States,
and declared the fourth Thursday of every November as "a day
of Thanksgiving." Think you know who he was? Really?

Every grade-schooler thinks he or she knows the answer. If you
immediately think of a dollar bill and the capital of our country,
or "the father of our country" and answer "George Washington,"
you would be . . . incorrect. You might be thinking to yourself, *Is
this some sort of trick?* No, it is true. George Washington was not
our first president. In this quirk of American history, the facts
actually contradict what we've always assumed was true.

George Washington was the first elected president under our Constitution and assumed office in 1789. But the United States had been a nation since the 13 colonies adopted the Articles of Confederation in 1781. Congress then promptly and unanimously elected the first president of the United States, and his name was John Hanson. He served as president for only one year but, interestingly, a colleague of Hanson's wrote him a personal note that read, "I congratulate your Excellency on your appointment to fill the most important seat in the United States." That note was signed by George Washington.

Even though we may never have heard that John Hanson was the first president of the United States, it's the truth. You may not even like it, but it is history.

And even though you may never have heard or understood that Jesus Christ, the Son of God, gave his life as a sacrificial payment for our sin, it's the truth.

And now, having heard that truth, whether you should choose to investigate it and accept it, or completely ignore it, certainly doesn't change it one iota. Whether you accept it or reject it, it's still the truth. And what you do with that truth means everything.

—*Dan Stuecher*

Society today says that truth is a personal choice—what is truth to you may not be truth to another. What are your thoughts on this idea?

_____

_____

_____

_____

_____

_____

_____

_____

_____

_____

_____

_____

_____

_____

Jesus said that *he* was the truth. Do you believe that? Why or why not?

_____

_____

_____

_____

_____

_____

_____

_____

_____

_____

_____

_____

_____

_____

_____

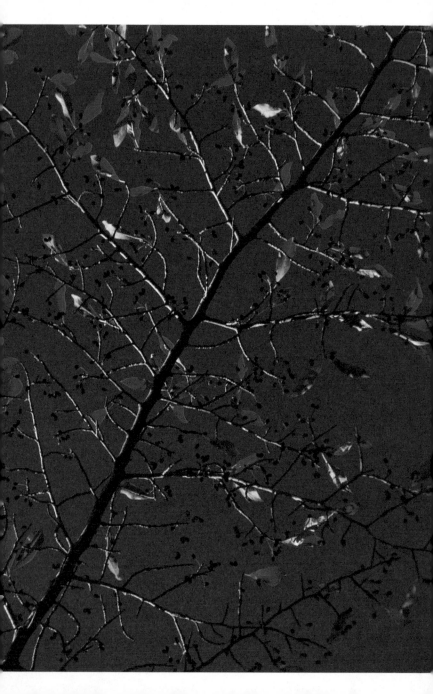

God with a Disability

He was pierced for our transgressions,

he was crushed for our iniquities;

the punishment that brought us peace was upon him,

and by his wounds we are healed.

ISAIAH 53:5

GOD WITH A DISABILITY

His name is James. He doesn't speak, but he does hum. Often it's a nameless tune. But sometimes he hums one unmistakable melody—"Jesus loves me, this I know, for the Bible tells me so."

James spent most of his early life in a state hospital. There, receiving little stimulation, encouragement, or personal care, he languished. But then he and seven other individuals with disabilities moved to an intermediate care facility. There he receives love, care, and encouragement. He attends church with a family from the community. He smiles warmly, hums that familiar tune, and you know James understands. He has a disability, but he knows someone else who had one too—God himself.

When Jesus was raised from the dead, the disciples might have expected the nail wounds in his hands and feet and the sword wound in his side to be healed. But they were not. I imagine some of the disciples thought the sight of those wounds was too much to bear. Perhaps they turned their eyes away from the torn and mangled flesh. But Jesus offered the sight to them as an opportunity to know the truth.

One disciple actually *wanted* to see those wounds. Thomas wouldn't believe Jesus was raised from the dead until he saw them. That sight brought him to his knees as he cried out, "My Lord and my God!" (John 20:28).

Jesus was there in all his resurrected power. He had defeated death—the only human ever to accomplish that feat. And yet, he still had wounds. He is a God with visible wounds; a God with, if you will, a disability. Jesus is God suffering with us in the midst of our suffering—sharing our wounds, our disabilities. I think James understands that. No wonder he sings.

—*Paul S. Williams*

What are your disabilities—mental, physical, spiritual? Write
them down here.

How does your perspective on your weaknesses change when you think that Jesus has gone through the same things and that he understands your struggles?

Write a prayer, giving your disabilities and weaknesses to the
Lord, knowing that he understands and is there to help you.

117

Deep Waters

*If the L*ORD* had not been on our side . . .*

the flood would have engulfed us,

the torrent would have swept over us,

the raging waters

would have swept us away. . . .

*Our help is in the name of the L*ORD*,*

the Maker of heaven and earth.

PSALM 124:2, 4, 5, 8

DEEP WATERS

When I was a child I used to play in the lake at Carter Caves State Park in eastern Kentucky. The swimming area was fenced off and lifeguards were everywhere; but still, Mom kept a watchful eye on my brother and me as we dog-paddled toward the deep-water marker. If we got too close to the marker, Mom gave us a call back. It's what mothers do.

We often went with our cousins. Aunt Lela, their mother, was a good woman. She had a great listening ear. But she had this thing about water. As soon as her daughters got their ankles wet, Aunt Lela was yelling at them to come back toward the shore. If they got the top of their bathing suits wet at all, it was purely by accident. She just didn't want them venturing into the deep.

We were at the lake once when I was about five. We traveled in a jeep wagon that friends of my father were taking to the mission field in what is now Zimbabwe. I imagined the jeep bouncing across the African plains, lions in hot pursuit. Evidently Mom and Aunt Lela had thought about those lions as well. They were nervous about the well-being of their friends. One missionary was a physician. Certainly he could find a wonderful job here, Aunt Lela said. Why did they have to go all the way to Africa? But go to Africa they did, and I do believe they "got their bathing suits wet." We all do sooner or later, whether our mothers like it or not.

All three of my children have been "swimming on their own" for some time now. They still look back to the shore every now and again, and that's where my job comes in. I yell that the way ahead looks inviting, and I assure them they have the strength to get back to the shore if necessary. Most of all, I let them know I'll still be there when they return.

Here's the story of another mother and child. He was her Son, but she never really understood him. He was never home. He left the family caravan once and headed off on his own. And then came the worst blow of all. He took off swimming in deep water way over his head, and there would be no coming home. He became a wanted man from one territory to the next. The authorities finally caught up with him and he was sent to trial. It would almost have been easier if she had never known, but they came and told her, and with her heart in her throat she traveled right into the middle of Hell.

Her Son was sentenced to death. He was convicted at a sham of a trial before a puppet judge, but there was nothing she could do but watch. It was more than she could bear, but she couldn't leave her Son. She followed him across the dusty streets, out through the city gates, and into the Place of the Skull. And there they crucified him and he died. The mother looked upon her Son's lifeless eyes, all her questions unanswered, and all hope utterly lost.

But then, three days later, there was the resurrection. And I imagine that same mother laughed and cried and danced as no one had ever danced before. And because of that resurrection, mothers until the end of time will gladly encourage their sons and daughters to go into the deep, because the God who made the universe resides there.

—*Paul S. Williams*

What "deep waters" have you been afraid to venture into, even though you know it's a risk God is asking you to take?

_____

_____

_____

_____

_____

_____

_____

_____

_____

_____

_____

_____

_____

_____

_____

What is the worst that could happen if you took this leap of faith? What is the best that might happen if you follow God's leading?

_____

_____

_____

_____

_____

_____

_____

_____

_____

_____

_____

_____

_____

Such As It Is?

But whatever was to my profit I now consider loss for the sake of Christ. What is more, I consider everything a loss compared to the surpassing greatness of knowing Christ Jesus my Lord, for whose sake I have lost all things. I consider them rubbish, that I may gain Christ and be found in him, not having a righteousness of my own that comes from the law, but that which is through faith in Christ—the righteousness that comes from God and is by faith. I want to know Christ and the power of his resurrection and the fellowship of sharing in his sufferings, becoming like him in his death, and so, somehow, to attain to the resurrection from the dead.

PHILIPPIANS 3:7-11

SUCH AS IT IS?

I have a good friend who commented once after a relative's con-version to the Christian faith, "It was nice seeing her come to faith and all, such as it is."

"Such as it is?" I asked.

"Well, I'm not sure how much is really there," was his reply. "I don't put much stock in the biblical account of history. But I guess faith does provide some meaning and comfort."

He is not my only friend who feels that way. I know many others who have relegated Christian faith to a back burner of their lives, speaking of it in "such as it is" kinds of tones. But is that all there is to Christianity? Is it a cultural hand-me-down with-out much real substance, providing some modest spiritual return, "such as it is"? Or is it something more?

Many have a nominal Christian heritage but readily admit their faith carries little meaning in their everyday lives. Most of them are truly glad my faith is deeply meaningful to me. "I'm glad you've found your spiritual grounding," they say, "but it's not my story."

That is how they understand the spiritual journey. Religious beliefs are just preferences, like one's favorite color or favorite seafood restaurant. There is no right or wrong, just "what is right for me."

While I respect my friends, I believe there *is* a universal story intended for all. It is a true story that happened at an ascertainable time and place in the past. It is not a made-up story. This story has been delivered to us by God the creator. It is the story of how God desires to reconcile the entire creation to himself, and its central focus is a point in history captured by a symbol—a wooden cross.

The Christian story is outrageous. God came to Earth to live as a man among us. He lived a life of love without fail. He was nailed to a cross and killed by his enemies, and three days later he was resurrected from the grave. That, I believe, is the focal point of human history. It is the story that changes everything. It is the story that says there is a future for the human race, and there is a future for me beyond death.

You are completely free to reject this story, and many will. You are free to put it on a back burner in your life, where it will bring a little comfort, "such as it is." Or you can make the death and resurrection of Jesus the focal point of your life, as God made it the focal point of human history. The cross can be the defining symbol of your life's story.

The choice is yours.

—Paul S. Williams

What role does Christ play in your life? Is he the center or just
a man whose story you heard in church as a kid? Why does he
have that role?

What do you think it means to make Christ the focal point of your life?

_____

_____

_____

_____

_____

_____

129

_____

_____

_____

_____

_____

_____

_____

Halloween Hype

We fix our eyes not on what is seen, but on what is unseen. For what is seen is temporary, but what is unseen is eternal.

2 CORINTHIANS 4:18

HALLOWEEN HYPE

You can love it; you can hate it. You can attribute it to the demonic; use it as a gauge for just how far we have strayed spiritually in our culture; or call it innocent fun for the kids, totally undeserving of the criticism of right-wing fundamentalists. I'm talking about Halloween. Your feelings probably fit somewhere in the spectrum I described. So what's the point of it all?

What we call Halloween goes back 2,500 years to the Celtic calendar when summer officially ended on October 31. The holiday was called Samhain—the Celtic New Year. Over centuries Catholicism blended this tradition and the rituals associated with it into their All Saints Day or All Hallows Eve on November 1, in large part because the seasonal timing coincided with the celebration of the year's harvest.

The custom of Halloween didn't make it to America until the 1840s, when Irish immigrants escaping the potato famine brought with them the various practices associated with the ancient celebration.

The jack-o'-lantern originated in the folklore of Britain. Trick or Treat started with the ninth century practice called "souling" when Christians walked from village to village begging for "soul cakes." The more soul cakes they received, the more prayers they promised to offer on behalf of the dead relatives of the donors.

Even though what we call Halloween is a far cry from the Celtic celebration that came into being 500 years before Jesus, there is one benefit to modern Halloween, if we have eyes to see it.

Halloween's focus on the supernatural reminds us of one truth we are often lulled into avoiding. That truth is that we are spiritual beings first, physical ones second. The physical world is temporary. The spiritual is eternal. Life is a spiritual matter. Our personal identity is a spiritual matter. Our destiny is a spiritual matter. The ancients knew this. However, their limited understanding and fear led them into great confusion and wild speculation. They were left to sort out spiritual matters the best they could until God revealed himself through his Son and his Word. Even then, old customs held on tenaciously. You witness that on Halloween night.

This year as you pass out the candy to all the cute little ghosts, goblins, and cartoon characters you see at your door, remember that God has indeed created us in his spiritual image. Although the holiday may be shallow, let it serve as a reminder that our spiritual destiny rests on the basis of what we choose to do with the one whom the English called "The Holy Ghost" and who called himself "the Way, the Truth, and the Life" (see John 14:6).

—*Dan Stuecher*

What do you think about Halloween? Why do you think you feel
the way you do?

_____

_____

_____

_____

_____

_____

_____

_____

_____

_____

_____

_____

_____

What does it mean in your life to know that you are a spiritual being with an eternal destiny? Are you sure of what your destiny will be at the end of this life?

135

Cleansing Blood and the English Language

The law requires that nearly everything be cleansed with blood,
and without the shedding of blood there is no forgiveness. . . .
Christ was sacrificed once to take away the sins of many people;
and he will appear a second time, not to bear sin, but to bring
salvation to those who are waiting for him.

HEBREWS 9:22, 28

CLEANSING BLOOD AND THE ENGLISH LANGUAGE

I remember hearing more than once that English is among the most difficult of the world's languages to learn. It ranks right up there with Chinese and Russian.

One of the complexities of English is that, frequently, a single word can be used in a variety of ways. For example, a recent article in the Florida newspaper, the *St. Petersburg Times*, told of the alarming discovery that local blood supplies were tainted with the HIV virus. It went on to describe extensive efforts to assure the public that the problem could be completely resolved. Being a blood donor myself, the article was certainly of interest to me. But it was the headline that caught my attention, and it illustrates my point about the English language. It read:

Cleansing Blood Comes at a High Price

The headline and accompanying article went on to highlight the expensive precautions being implemented to make sure blood supplies were free of the deadly HIV virus. The writer appropriately used the word *cleansing* as a verb. To me, however, the headline conveyed a very different message. You see, I read the word *cleansing* as an adjective. "Cleansing Blood Comes at a High Price." When I saw those words on the front page of a liberal newspaper I was stunned! Everything else disappeared!

Even though I had fallen victim to one of the many nuances of the English language, I was deeply touched and immediately reminded that the blood necessary to cleanse me from the ugliness of sin came at the incredibly high price of God's Son being sacrificed on a forbidding hill called Calvary. "Cleansing Blood Comes at a High Price."

The cleansing blood of Jesus accomplished what nothing else could. It took away the nasty stain of sin in my life. God and I were on opposite sides of a wall. But Jesus, dying as an expression of God's justice and mercy, broke down the wall and washed me completely clean. I'm forgiven and need never again fear separation from my heavenly Father. Instead of having to pay the penalty for sin with my own life, I can accept that Jesus made the payment in full by offering *his* life in place of mine! Rather than being alienated from God, I have actually been adopted into his family! I can't tell you how refreshed I was from reading that newspaper headline incorrectly. I was also prompted to reflect that, should he choose to do so, God could encode subtle reminders of his love for us anytime he chooses— in the most unlikely places.

So, if you'll excuse me, I'm going to see if there are any exciting messages he may have hidden in today's paper. . . .

—*Dan Stuecher*

139

If you had come across the headline "Cleansing Blood Comes at a High Price" in your local paper, what would you think? What would your first thought be?

_____

_____

_____

_____

_____

_____

_____

_____

_____

_____

_____

_____

Have you ever had a similar experience—seeing a reminder of God's love in an unlikely place? How does it make you feel about God, knowing that he uses simple things like a newspaper headline to speak to us of his grace?

_____

_____

_____

_____

_____

_____

_____

_____

_____

_____

_____

_____

_____

Hope for Cracked Pots

This is the word that came to Jeremiah from the LORD:

"Go down to the potter's house, and there I will give you

my message."

So I went down to the potter's house, and I saw him working at

the wheel. But the pot he was shaping from the clay was marred

in his hands; so the potter formed it into another pot, shaping it

as seemed best to him.

Then the word of the LORD came to me: "O house of Israel, can

I not do with you as this potter does?" declares the LORD. "Like

clay in the hand of the potter, so are you in my hand, O house

of Israel."

JEREMIAH 18:1-6

HOPE FOR CRACKED POTS

I was having lunch with David, and I was just about to order but-termilk pie. David has a lot of questions—questions about life being fair, questions regarding the guilt he feels over bad deci-sions, questions about God. I love questions, and I like David, so I asked him to come to church to see if he'd find some answers. Now I really didn't think that any one church service would relieve his guilt or solve his dilemmas. I just wanted him to be exposed to an atmosphere where God might make himself real to David.

Well, the waitress brought the buttermilk pie, but it just sat for a while. There was something more important to chew on first. David really wanted answers to his questions and relief for his guilt, but he just didn't want to come into a church. To be more accurate, David really did want to come, but he felt as if he weren't good enough to be there. He said, "All those other good people would not want a terrible person like me in their church."

Wow. I've heard about people who believed that, but this was the first real live one I'd ever met.

David was looking for hope in a life that was wracked by guilt, so much guilt that he felt unworthy to even be inside a church building. I suppose you could say that he didn't think his imper-fection would be accepted among supposedly "perfect" people.

Well, David and I enjoyed some buttermilk pie, and I tried to give him a glimmer of hope. That glimmer required David to envision a clay pot in the hands of a potter. The pot was marred, cracked, and in need of a touch from the potter's skilled hands. The potter applied a little water to the hardened clay, just enough water to moisten the dry cracked pot. He then touched and molded the clay as only a trained professional could. The potter restored an imperfect pot to its intended condition. I wanted David to see himself as the pot and God as the potter. If he could do that, I knew he would no longer be afraid to attend church. And furthermore, he'd know that everyone in the church is really just a broken pot in the hands of the master potter.

The picture of the pot and the potter is not original to me—it is God's story written by Jeremiah in chapter 18 of his book. The hope of the story is found in the phrase: "the pot . . . was marred in his hands." The hope of the story is that, although the pot was imperfect, it was still in the hands of the potter. The hope for David is that, even though he has made some dreadful mistakes with his marriage, his children, and his life, the master potter has not discarded him. God does not throw us away when we make mistakes. He can apply the water of his Holy Spirit and moisten us enough to relieve our guilt and forgive our bad choices as only he can. There is hope for cracked pots. In fact, we're the only kind of pots there are.

—Greg Allen

Do you feel like a cracked pot—full of imperfections, useless, ugly? What things in your life make you feel that way?

_____

_____

_____

_____

_____

_____

_____

_____

_____

_____

_____

_____

_____

_____

How does it change your perspective to realize that we are *all* cracked pots and that God is still working on us, to make us into the shape he wants?

A Merry Christmas to All

And there were shepherds living out in the fields nearby, keeping watch over their flocks at night. An angel of the Lord appeared to them, and the glory of the Lord shone around them, and they were terrified. But the angel said to them, "Do not be afraid. I bring you good news of great joy that will be for all the people. Today in the town of David a Savior has been born to you; he is Christ the Lord. . . ."

When the angels had left them and gone into heaven, the shepherds said to one another, "Let's go to Bethlehem and see this thing that has happened, which the Lord has told us about." So they hurried off and found Mary and Joseph, and the baby, who was lying in the manger.

Luke 2:8-11, 15, 16

A MERRY CHRISTMAS TO ALL

"And there were shepherds living out in the fields nearby, keeping watch over their flocks at night" (Luke 2:8). You know what I love about that part of the Christmas story? Common, ordinary people encountered God himself as they went about their normal, everyday living. That's what the Bible says—that the shepherds were "living" in the fields. Being a shepherd was no Fortune 500 CEO job—they were pulling third shift duty too, staying up at night to keep intruding wolves from attacking the sleeping sheep.

And yet these shepherds were about to see an angel of the Lord who would tell them the Savior of the world had just been born. They were the first to hear the news. And when they saw the angel from God they were scared to death. But the angel assured these workers that everything was OK, because the God of all creation had just come to Earth in the flesh. And the good news he would bring was not just for the elite. The good news of Christmas was for common, ordinary people, like them.

The audience that first heard the Christmas story was a blue-collar crowd, shepherds working long and hard hours in the most difficult of circumstances. But guess who else was let in on the Christmas story? The Fortune 500 elite of their day—we know them as the wise men. "Magi from the east came to Jerusalem and asked, 'Where is the one who has been born king of the Jews?'" (Matthew 2:1, 2). Magi, according to centuries of tradition, were kings. Their income was evidently thousands of times that of the shepherds.

And you know what I like about these particular wealthy wise men? They knew when to acknowledge someone mightier than they. They followed the star and made their way to honor a greater king. And when they finally arrived at Jesus' home, they were overjoyed. These men of position had made a simple pilgrimage. And as they laid eyes on the Christ-child, they bowed and worshiped, opened their treasures, and presented their gifts.

And so the story came to both common men and those of privilege. The good news about Jesus was a gift for all.

I love reading the Christmas story. It's for everybody—the rich and the poor. You know why? Because to Christ, we are all the same. He doesn't care about our money; he cares about our need. And what we all need has nothing to do with money. Our universal need is found in Luke 2:11—"Today in the town of David a Savior has been born to you; he is Christ the Lord."

The good news about Jesus is that he came to save everybody. He came to save us from a life lived without purpose and from holidays without meaning. He came to help the rich see they are poor, to help the poor see they are rich and to help us all see we are made for something far beyond what this world can ever offer—an eternity of bringing glory to God.

—Greg Allen

What does Christmas mean to you? How does the biblical account of Christ's birth affect you personally?

How might you bring the good news of Christmas into your life, and the lives of others, all year round?

_155_

grace

Anthony's Demons

At one time we too were foolish, disobedient, deceived and enslaved by all kinds of passions and pleasures. We lived in malice and envy, being hated and hating one another. But when the kindness and love of God our Savior appeared, he saved us, not because of righteous things we had done, but because of his mercy. He saved us through the washing of rebirth and renewal by the Holy Spirit, whom he poured out on us generously through Jesus Christ our Savior, so that, having been justified by his grace, we might become heirs having the hope of eternal life.

TITUS 3:3-7

ANTHONY'S DEMONS

I watched the crowd of thousands applaud the minister's sermon. He had done a very fine job. My applause was tepid. *I would have done better,* I kept thinking.

I picked up a best-selling book of stories at a chain store and leafed through the pages. *It's all right,* I thought. *But my book of stories is better. How come my book isn't on the shelf of every bookstore in the nation?*

I'll be honest. It's painful to admit those thoughts. But you understand them. We all understand envy, jealousy, and pride. Unfortunately, those things are never far from the surface.

Anthony of Egypt was a renowned spiritual leader. His long life spanned half of the third and fourth centuries. His popularity was responsible for the creation of thousands of monasteries. And his life story, recorded shortly after his death, reads like that of a superhero from a spiritual comic book. But Anthony was not immune to the envy, jealousy, and pride that plague us all.

When we think of the mythical wise-man-on-the-mountain, we are thinking of people like Anthony of Egypt. The famous monk lived in the desert to the age of 105 and spent much of his time, it seems, battling monstrous demons, which attacked him daily in the cave where he lived.

Supposedly, those who spent time with Anthony heard the shrieks and screams of the demons all through the night. During the Middle Ages, artists tried to paint Anthony's famous battles. They presented an old man being pummeled by grotesque and hideous creatures.

Anthony, like many church fathers, had come from a wealthy background. Upon deciding to follow Christ, however, he gave away his possessions and devoted his life to the pursuit of God and the service of others. But he struggled in his devotion and daily found himself battling those grotesque and hideous demons. What was that all about?

Anthony, Jerome, Athanasius, and Augustine were all fourth century church fathers who practiced the spiritual disciplines, including fasting, or not eating for a period of time—something quite common in their day. Fasting was practiced throughout the Bible. Even Jesus did it during his 40 days in the wilderness. It was not done to earn favor with God. It was a way to focus on God and allow him to transform the heart.

All the church fathers, including Anthony of Egypt, tell us that when one is fasting, the ugly parts of the personality tend to rise to the surface. Traits like pride, anger, bitterness, or lust. These hidden addictions, usually lurking just beneath the surface of our lives, raise their grotesque heads to capture and enslave us. Being revealed in this way allows these "demons" to be dealt with more directly.

Maybe it wasn't literal multi-fanged monsters that Anthony was fighting in his cave. Maybe it was something far worse. Maybe it was jealousy that others were more successful than he. Maybe it was envy that others had received more blessings. Maybe it was pride that he had been overlooked, instead of receiving the honor he thought he deserved. Maybe it was lust that invited him to take pleasure, without giving love in return.

We all fight demons, because sin is real, and it resides in us. But there is good news. God's love is greater than our demons. And if we will turn our hearts steadfastly to Christ, we too, like Anthony of Egypt, will see the love of God triumph over our shadow sides.

—Eric Snyder for Paul S. Williams

What "demons" do you struggle with? List them here.

_____

_____

_____

_____

_____

_____

_____

_____

_____

_____

_____

_____

_____

_____

_____

_____

Write a prayer, giving each of these things you struggle with to Jesus. He promises to forgive you and cleanse you of these "demons."

In Whom Do You Trust?

Some trust in chariots and some in horses,

but we trust in the name of the LORD our God.

PSALM 20:7

IN WHOM DO YOU TRUST?

In December 2001, Buffalo, New York, received 81.5 inches of snow in just five days. The huge storm caught the city by surprise. It had not been forecast at all. Upstate New Yorkers are accustomed to lake-effect snowstorms that pick up moisture from Lake Erie and drop it on western New York State. But this storm was far worse than expected. I imagine it will be a good long while before the folks in Buffalo trust their weather forecasters again. Maybe they'd rather listen to Punxsutawney Phil, the famous groundhog who predicts the length of winter each February 2. Maybe good old Phil could have predicted their wintry future.

Each year, thousands of people visit Punxsutawney, Pennsylvania, on Groundhog Day. The city began celebrating the day in 1887, and over the years it's become quite an event. The festivities begin early. By 3:00 in the morning buses are rolling into Gobbler's Knob. There, crowds enjoy music, entertainment, and even fireworks.

But the day belongs to Phil—the groundhog. He spends most of the year in his very own "Groundhog Zoo" at the Civic Complex in downtown Punxsutawney. But as the sun rises on Groundhog Day, a member of the Punxsutawney Groundhog Club hoists Phil into the air and announces his prediction to the gathered crowds.

People all over the world look to Phil each February and hope his predictions come true. He has posed for a picture with the Groundhog Day Queen, appeared on the *Today* show, visited the White House, and been a guest on *The Oprah Winfrey Show.* But no one ever seems to ask the obvious question. Just how accurate are Phil's weather predictions? Does he do any better than the forecasters in Buffalo?

In the last 116 years, Phil, the weather-predicting groundhog, has seen his shadow 93 times. Yet Phil has accurately predicted six more weeks of winter only 40 percent of the time. His track record leaves a little to be desired.

But Phil is not the only one whose crystal ball needs repairs. In 1943, the chairman of the board of IBM announced, "I think there is a world market for about five computers." A recording company expert predicted in 1962, "We don't think the Beatles will do anything in their market. Guitar groups are on the way out."

Throughout history, no matter how hard we try, we're not very good at predicting the future. Corrie Ten Boom, a concentration camp survivor, probably put it best: "Never be afraid to trust an unknown future to a knowing God."

— Jennifer Taylor for Rick Rusaw

Whom do you trust? Yourself? Your spouse? Your money? Why do you think you trust in those people or things?

What would it take for you to trust fully in God? How might that trust change your life?

_____

_____

_____

_____

_____

_____

_____

_____

_____

_____

_____

_____

_____

Covering Truth

We demolish arguments and every pretension that sets itself up

against the knowledge of God, and we take captive every thought

to make it obedient to Christ.

2 CORINTHIANS 10:5

COVERING TRUTH

"Ignorance is bliss."

"You can't get stressed over what you don't know."

"That's more information than I need."

"What you don't know can't hurt you."

I'm sure you will agree all of those statements are in error. What you don't know *can* hurt you. If you've ever had to pay a speeding ticket when you honestly didn't know the speed limit, you were most likely reminded, "Ignorance of the law is no excuse."

When it comes to our relationship with the living God, what we don't know can be eternally devastating. Let me tell a story that illustrates this point.

The year was 1902. The campaigns for the election in the town of Saint-Pierre, on the Caribbean island of Martinique, were heating up. The election was just days away. Unfortunately, also heating up was Pelée, the active volcano on the island. It was rumbling, smoking, and belching fire in a way few of the islanders had ever seen. Most everyone was growing uneasy. But the governor of the island, Louis Mouttet, was concerned that if people grew preoccupied with the volcano and stayed at home instead of venturing out to vote, it would hurt his political party in the election. So he told the newspaper not to mention the volcano. He actually blocked roads out of the city and refused to publicize telegrams warning of an eruption. He showed up in town just before the election to declare that everything was fine. I suppose you could say he kept his constituents "blissfully ignorant."

Writer Rick Beyer tells us that at 8:00 the morning after the governor arrived, Pelée erupted. A vast cloud of gas and volcanic ash, heated to 1,000 degrees, swept over the city at speeds approaching 100 miles per hour. In less than two minutes 30,000 people died and what had been a beautiful harbor city was nothing more than a smoking ruin. What you don't know can hurt you—it can even kill you.

We live in an age that would like nothing more than to completely cover up one particular truth. It is a rather simple truth, actually, but one many people, in the interest of tolerance and pluralism, choose to obstinately resist, if not dismiss altogether. There are more important things that deserve our attention, they say—like world peace, hunger, disease, or the environment. When it comes to this particular matter, a secular society has determined you're much better off ignoring it.

Jesus said, "I am the way and the truth and the life. No one comes to the Father except through me" (John 14:6). This is the truth that the world wants to ignore. For the life of me, I can't understand why this truth is seen as intolerant, and therefore inappropriate. It is not a threat of being excluded. It is an unbelievable invitation to be *included*—to be included among those God has reconciled to himself, to be included among those to whom he has offered eternal life.

So, it's up to you. You can ignore the smoking mountain. Or you can give it the attention it deserves. The choice is yours.

—Dan Stuecher

In your opinion, why do people see the gospel of Jesus as intolerant and politically incorrect? What are their reasons for wanting to ignore the message of the cross?

Do you agree with those who want to push Christianity aside because they feel it isn't appropriate? Why or why not?

_____

_____

_____

_____

_____

_____

_____

_____

_____

_____

_____

_____

_____

The Stranger Who Removed Shame

My guilt has overwhelmed me

> *like a burden too heavy to bear. . . .*

I wait for you, O LORD;

> *you will answer, O Lord my God. . . .*

I confess my iniquity;

> *I am troubled by my sin. . . .*

O LORD, do not forsake me;

> *be not far from me, O my God.*

Come quickly to help me,

> *O Lord my Savior.*

PSALM 38:4, 15, 18, 21, 22

THE STRANGER WHO REMOVED SHAME

The woman looked older than her years as she took her worn and battered body through the village streets into the desert to Jacob's well. It was a ritual she practiced late every morning. There was a closer well, but she wasn't welcome there, so she worked her tired way to this old well where brackish water bubbled up from the desert bottom.

A man was there, and he asked her for a drink. He was a Jew and she was a Samaritan. Jews didn't speak to Samaritans, so she asked him why he was talking to her in the first place (see John 4:4-30).

He didn't answer her question. He said, "If you knew who I was, you'd ask me for living water." Did he mean running water, like you find in a cool mountain stream? What she wouldn't give for a taste of that. He went on, "Drink this water and you'll be thirsty again. But drink of the living water I have, and you will never thirst again." She may have thought, *Great, this guy's flat out crazy.*

"So tell me," she said, "how're you going to get this water? You don't even have a bucket" (see John 4:11).

The man changed the subject. He said, "Go get your husband." She answered, "I don't have a husband." Then the man spoke again, and what he said changed everything.

The man said, "I know you don't have a husband. You've had five before, and the man you're living with now isn't your husband." And with that, her secret was out. And she was filled with guilt.

I think there are at least two different kinds of cultures in the world—shame cultures and guilt cultures. In shame culture the worst possible thing is to lose face, to *appear* bad before your peers. Modern American gangs and some historical Asian cultures are shame cultures. The question isn't about right or wrong. The question is about looking bad in front of your friends.

But in guilt culture, the worst possible thing is not losing face. The worst possible thing is to be found guilty of having *done* wrong. To violate your conscience and destroy your relationships is a terrible sin. And that is what this woman had done.

But Jesus talked with her. He listened. I can imagine the conversation. Maybe she'd been with six different men because her father abandoned her when she was a young child, and she was going to abandon others before they could abandon her. That would explain five marriages. Or maybe she was abused and didn't feel she'd ever be able to trust a man again. That would explain it as well. But *this* man didn't condemn. He listened and gave her hope. And they talked. He said to focus on God and on the truth. And she heard him, right down to her heart. And finally, when her secrets were revealed to this wise man who listened with acceptance and love, her guilt was broken.

By the time these two were finished speaking, she was a hopeful woman. She went back into town and told everyone what happened. "I met a man," she said, "who knew everything I ever did." And she said it in a way that let them know they had to rush out to meet this strange Jewish man who uncovered secrets and removed guilt.

And the same stranger has been helping folks move beyond guilt and shame for 2,000 years. All you have to do is find the courage to tell him your secrets. He already knows them anyway . . . and he loves you just the same.

—*Paul S. Williams*

Are you hiding secrets of shame and guilt? Why? What are those secrets doing to you inside?

_____

_____

_____

_____

_____

_____

_____

_____

_____

_____

_____

_____

_____

God already knows your secrets. Take the first step toward healing and write them out here as a prayer, giving them into God's
loving hands.

_____

_____

_____

_____

_____

_____

_____

_____

_____

_____

_____

_____

_____

What Do You Ask of Me?

I heard the voice of the Lord saying, "Whom shall I send? And who will go for us?"

And I said, "Here am I. Send me!"

ISAIAH 6:8

WHAT DO YOU ASK OF ME?

I hate to admit it, but my chart at the doctor's office is mighty thick. Now it's important to understand I've never been seriously ill. And for the last 10 years or so, I've been a normal guy, which translated means, I might go to the doctor after both arms have fallen off. But through my 20s and 30s, I was at the doctor's office every other Thursday—always sure I was gravely ill. Every pinched nerve was some awful neurological disease. Every tiny ache was a hidden, life-threatening illness. Both my family doctors are friends of mine. They just rolled their eyes. But my most hidden illness during those years wasn't physical at all.

I came to realize I was sick all right, but there was nothing physical about it. My sickness was my need to keep convincing myself that I was in total control of my life—that I was in charge. So the very possibility of debilitating diseases that would cause me to lose control of myself was simply unacceptable.

You don't get very far in life living under that illusion of control. Eventually you have to swallow hard and give up the fantasy that you are in charge of your own future. And when you finally give up that impossible burden, you open yourself up to a brave new world.

Kathleen Norris tells of a 16th century monk who, while deep in a debilitating illness, prayed a single prayer over and over again: "Father, what do you ask of me?"

It takes a tremendous trust in God to be able to pray that prayer. And implied in the saying is a complete and utter confidence that God can be trusted, no matter the outcome.

The journey then, in spite of difficulties, becomes an adventure in trust, a ride to be embraced. Though we have no idea about the twists and turns on the way, we do know where the ride will end. It ends where it began—in the arms of our creator.

I still don't have the faith of that monk. Not yet, anyway. But I am learning to give up the fantasy that I control my own destiny. I'm learning to live my life one day at a time, never knowing what's around the next bend. I'm learning to embrace the mystery. And I do hope I can grow into the courage to say, "Father, I trust you completely. Now, what do you ask of me?"

—Paul S. Williams

What areas of your life do you work hard to control? What happens when you find you can't control those things the way you want to? Pray on paper, asking God to help you give up control to him. He controls the universe. Ask him to help you to have the courage to ask, "What do you ask of me, Lord?"

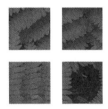

Devotions in this book are based on scripts first delivered by Paul S. Williams and the following hosts for *Worship*.

Greg Allen is a worship minister at Southeast Christian Church in Louisville, Kentucky, where he has served since 1983.

Rick Rusaw is senior minister at LifeBridge Christian Church in Longmont, Colorado, where he has served since 1991.

Dan Stuecher is senior minister at Harborside Christian Church in Safety Harbor, Florida, a congregation he founded in 1984.